AIR FORCE SUPPLEMENT TO THE DEPARTMENT OF DEFENSE DICTIONARY OF MILITARY AND ASSOCIATED TERMS

Air Force Doctrine Document 1-02
11 January 2007

Incorporating Change 1, 6 January 2012

This document supplements the terminology in Joint Publication 1-02,
Department of Defense Dictionary of Military and Associated Terms

BY ORDER OF THE
SECRETARY OF THE AIR FORCE

AIR FORCE DOCTRINE DOCUMENT 1-02
11 JANUARY 2007
INCORPORATING CHANGE 1, 6 JANUARY 2012 |

SUMMARY OF CHANGES

This Interim change to Air Force Doctrine Document (AFDD) 1-02, *Air Force Supplement to the Department of Defense Dictionary of Military and Associated Terms* updates reference publications, abbreviations, and definitions. It also updates the number of this AFDD from 1-2 to 1-02, coinciding with the *Department of Defense Dictionary of Military and Associated Terms*. A margin bar indicates newly revised material.

Supersedes: AFDD 1-2, 8 June 2006
OPR: LeMay Center/DDS
Certified by: LeMay Center/DD
Pages: 65
Accessibility: Available on the e-publishing website at www.e-publishing.af.mil for
          downloading
Releasability: There are no releasability restrictions on this publication
Approved by: LeMay Center/CC, Maj Gen Thomas K. Andersen, USAF
          Commander, LeMay Center for Doctrine Development and Education

FOREWORD

Airmen require a lexicon of unique military terms to include agreed upon definitions, acronyms, and abbreviations. This lexicon enhances the clear articulation of thoughts, ideas and commands through a common operational language fundamental to the application of airpower. AFDD 1-02 is the Air Force supplement to Joint Publication 1-02, the Department of Defense Dictionary of Military and Associated Terms. This living document presents Service-unique terminology, highlighting the Airmen's perspective, and will evolve as terms and definitions evolve.

Thomas K. Andersen
Major General, USAF
Commander, LeMay Center for Doctrine
Development and Education

TABLE OF CONTENTS

INTRODUCTION

PURPOSE

This publication has been prepared under the direction of the Chief of Staff of the United States Air Force. It implements Department of Defense Directive 5025.12, *Standardization of Military and Associated Terminology*, which directs the use of Joint Publication 1-02, *Department of Defense Dictionary of Military and Associated Terms*, throughout the Department of Defense to ensure uniformity in the use of terms and definitions.

The *Air Force Supplement to the DOD Dictionary of Military and Associated Terms* is a living document to be used in conjunction with JP 1-02, the DOD Dictionary and AAP-6, NATO Glossary of Terms and Definitions.

APPLICATION

This AFDD applies to all Air Force military and civilian personnel, including regular, Air Force Reserve, and Air National Guard units and members. Unless specifically stated otherwise, Air Force doctrine applies to the full range of military operations.

The doctrinal terminology in this document is authoritative, but not directive. Therefore, commanders need to consider the contents of this AFDD and the particular situation when accomplishing their missions. Airmen should read it, discuss it, and practice it.

SCOPE

The *Air Force Supplement to the DOD Dictionary of Military and Associated Terms* lists terminology that has been standardized for use within the US Air Force. It is a consolidated list of terms, definitions, abbreviations, and acronyms from all approved AFDDs, as well as terms and definitions from other publications with broad application. **It does not contain terminology that duplicates entries in JP 1-02 unless there is a need for clarity.** In that circumstance, the JP 1-02 definition will be followed by an Air Force-clarity statement.

As Air Force doctrinal terms are approved through AFDDs, they will be added to the glossary. Other Air Force terms meeting the requirement may be added as requested. Users can gain access to the living glossary by accessing the LeMay Center's web site at: *https://wwwmil.maxwell.af.mil/au/lemay/doctrine.htm.*

CHAPTER ONE

AIR FORCE TERMINOLOGY STANDARDIZATION PROGRAM

OBJECTIVE

The objective of the Air Force Terminology Standardization Program is to enhance communication through a common understanding of terms and definitions that are of general military or associated significance.

STANDARDIZATION PROGRAM

The Air Force participates in terminology standardization at the unilateral, joint, and multinational levels. Collectively, these programs are referred to as the Air Force Military Terminology Standardization Program.

Air Force

The Air Force Military Terminology Standardization Program provides terminology unique to the Air Force mission. Approved terms, definitions, abbreviations, and acronyms are published in the *Air Force Supplement to the DOD Dictionary of Military and Associated Terms*. Doctrine terms and definitions are added as Air Force Doctrine Documents are written, revised, and approved. Other Air Force terms are added as requested and approved. The living glossary will be updated and can be accessed at the LeMay Center's web site at: https://wwwmil.maxwell.af.mil /au/lemay/doctrine.htm.

Joint

The DOD terminology standardization program is carried out under the direction of the Joint Chiefs of Staff, in coordination with the Office of the Secretary of Defense, the Military Services, and the Defense Agencies. Approved terms and definitions are published in JP 1-02, Department of Defense Dictionary of Military and Associated Terms. This publication can be accessed from the Joint Doctrine home page web site: https://jdeis.js.mil/jdeis/index.jsp .

North Atlantic Treaty Organization (NATO)

The NATO terminology standardization effort is an integral part of an overall NATO Standardization Program administered by the NATO Military Committee. The United States is a signatory to NATO Standardization Agreement (STANAG) 3860. Under the provisions of STANAG 3860, AAP-6, *NATO Glossary of Terms and Definitions,* is established as the authoritative NATO terminology reference, and member nations agree to use the terms and definitions published therein.

RESPONSIBILITIES

The Air Force Terminologist will:

○ Manage the Air Force Military Terminology Standardization Program by providing for its central direction, policy development, control and administration.

○ Maintain a comprehensive knowledge of military terminology standards, Air Force regulations, DOD directives, NATO regulations and other appropriate federal directives effecting current and proposed USAF terminology.

○ Represent the USAF in DOD and international terminology standardization conferences and meetings.

○ Review all USAF -level publications with glossaries for terminology standardization.

○ Coordinate, develop, and document the USAF position on terminology proposals from the DOD and international communities.

○ Compile proposals to change the *Air Force Supplement to the DOD Dictionary of Military and Associated Terms* (also known as the *Air Force Glossary*).

○ Maintain all USAF terminology standardization databases, programs, and regulations.

Commanders at all echelons will:

○ Ensure terms, definitions, abbreviations, and acronyms used in USAF publications are consistent with terminology in this document and Joint Pub 1-02.

○ Submit proposals to change the *Air Force Glossary* in accordance with procedures outlined in this publication.

○ Submit US Air Force-level publications with glossaries to the Air Force Terminologist via (LeMay Center/CC Workflow) for coordination in accordance with Air Force Instruction (AFI) 33-360, *Publications and Forms Management*.

CHAPTER TWO

REVISIONS AND CHANGES

CHANGES TO THE AIR FORCE *SUPPLEMENT TO THE DOD DICTIONARY OF MILITARY AND ASSOCIATED TERMS*

The *Air Force Supplement to the DOD Dictionary of Military and Associated Terms* is a living document and can be accessed at the LeMay Center *https://wwwmil. maxwell.af.mil /au/lemay/doctrine.htm.*

Changes will be posted periodically to the on-line version of this supplement and will normally occur in conjunction with the approval of AFDDs.

Proposals for changes to this supplement outside of the normal AFDD development process may be submitted to the USAF Terminologist on a limited basis. Changes will be approved in this manner only when there is not an applicable AFDD in development. Table 1.1 contains the criteria for the three types of proposed actions. Proposals should include the elements listed in Table 1.2. The Air Force Terminologist will consolidate proposals and present them to LeMay Center/DD in accordance with AFI 10-1301, *Air Force Doctrine*.

Table 1.1. Criteria for Proposed Terminology Actions.

ACTION	CRITERIA
Add	• Term is not adequately defined in a standard dictionary or JP 1-02. • Term is of general USAF significance. A technical or specialized term should be proposed only if it can be defined in easily understood language and its inclusion is of general importance.
Modify	• Term is incorrectly defined in the *Air Force Glossary*.
Delete	• Term is adequately defined in a standard dictionary. • Term has been defined in JP 1-02. • Term is of a technical or specialized nature and is not defined in easily understood language.

Table 1.2. Elements of a Proposal.

ELEMENT	INFORMATION
Action	See Table 1.1.
Criteria	See Table 1.1.
"Proposed" term and definition, acronym, or abbreviation	Definitions should not contain abbreviations, acronyms, or the term itself.
Source	AFDDs; Air Force publications
Rationale	Justification for the action.
Originator	Point of contact, organization, phone, fax.

GLOSSARY

ABBREVIATIONS

A1	personnel directorate (COMAFFOR)
A2	intelligence directorate (COMAFFOR)
A3	operations directorate (COMAFFOR)
A4	logistics directorate (COMAFFOR)
A5	plans directorate (COMAFFOR)
A6	communications directorate (COMAFFOR)
A7	installations and mission support (COMAFFOR)
A8	programs and financial management (COMAFFOR)
A9	analysis and assessments (COMAFFOR)
AAC	Air Armaments Center
AADC	area air defense commander
AADP	area air defense plan
ABS	air base squadron
ACA	airspace control authority
ACC	Air Combat Command
ACDE	aircrew chemical defense ensemble
ACF	analysis, correlation, and fusion
ACFT	analysis, correlation, and fusion team
ACL	allowable cabin loads
ACO	airspace control order
ACR	agile combat repair
ACS	agile combat support
ACT	aerial combat tactics
ADAPT	Alcohol and Drug Abuse Prevention and Treatment
ADCON	administrative control
ADSC	active duty service commitment
AE	aeromedical evacuation
AEC	aeromedical evacuation crew
AECT	aeromedical evaluation control team
AED	air expeditionary detachment

AEF	air expeditionary force
AEFC	Air Expeditionary Force Center
AEG	air expeditionary group
AERPS	aircrew eye and respiratory protection system
AES	air expeditionary squadron
AESC	aeromedical evacuation support cell
AETACS	airborne elements of the theater air control system
AETC	Air Education and Training Command
AETF	air expeditionary task force
AEW	Air Expeditionary Wing
AFAC	airborne forward air control
AFAUX	Air Force Auxiliary
AFB	Air Force base
AFCENT	Air Forces Central
AFCERT	Air Force computer emergency response team
AFCW	Aerospace Future Capabilities Wargame
AFDD	Air Force doctrine document
AFFOR	Air Force forces
AFI	Air Force instruction
AFIMS	Air Force Incident Management System
AFIOC	Air Force Information Operations Center
AFISRA	Air Force Intelligence, Surveillance and Reconnaissance Agency
AFIWC	Air Force Information Warfare Center
AFLE	Air Force liaison element
AFMETL	Air Force mission essential task list
AFMLOC	Air Force Medical Logistics Operation Center
AFMS	Air Force Medical Service
AFMSS	Air Force Mission Support System
AFNETOPS	Air Force network operations
AFNOC	Air Force Network Operations Center
AFNORTH	Air Forces Northern
AFNOSC	Air Force network operations security center

AFNSEP	Air Force National Security Emergency Preparedness Agency
AFOG	Air Force Operations Group
AFOSI	Air Force Office of Special Investigations
AFPAC	Air Forces Pacific
AFPD	Air Force policy directive
AFRAT	Air Force radiation assessment team
AFRC	Air Force Reserve Command
AFRL	Air Force Research Lab
AFSC	Air Force specialty code
AFSCN	Air Force Satellite Control Network
AFSOC	Air Force Special Operations Command
AFSOD	Air Force special operations detachment
AFSOE	Air Force special operations element
AFSOF	Air Force special operations forces
AFSP	Air Force Strategic Plan
AFSPC	Air Force Space Command
AFSPC/CC	Commander, Air Force Space Command
AFSST	Air Force space support team
AFSWC	Air Force Service Watch Cell
AFT	Air Force task
AFTL	Air Force Task List
AFTTP	Air Force tactics, techniques, and procedures
AG	aerial gunner
AGE	aerospace ground equipment
AGM	air-to-ground missile
AHO	above highest obstacle
AI	air interdiction
AIA	Air Intelligence Agency
AIE	alternate insertion/extraction
AIG	air intelligence group
AIM	air intercept missile
AIS	air intelligence squadron

ALC	air logistics center
ALCF	airlift control flight
ALCM	air launched cruise missile
ALCT	airlift control team
ALERTORD	alert order
ALLOREQ	allocation request
ALO	air liaison officer
ALSA	Air Land Sea Application Center
ALTRV	altitude reservation
ALZ	assault landing zones
AMC	Air Mobility Command
AMCT	air mobility control team
AMD	air mobility division
AMEGS	aircraft maintenance event ground station
AMLO	air mobility liaison officer
AMOCC	air mobility operations control center
AMOG	air mobility operations group
AMOS	air mobility operations squadron
AMS	air mobility squadron
AMT	air mobility team
AMX	air mobility express
ANG	Air National Guard
ANR	Alaska NORAD Region
AO	area of operations
AOC	air operations center
AOD	air operations directive
AOG	air operations group
AOR	area of responsibility
APF	aerial port flight
APOD	aerial port of debarkation
APOE	aerial port of embarkation
APS	aerial port squadron

AR	air refueling
ARC	Air Reserve Component
ARCT	air refueling control team
ARMS	Aviation Resource Management System
ARRS	air rescue and recovery service
ARW	air refueling wing
ASC	air support center
ASIC	Air and Space Interoperability Council
ASMT	aeromedical evacuation stage management team
ASOC	air support operations center
ASR	airport surveillance radar
ATC	air traffic control
ATD	aircrew training device
ATO	air tasking order
AU	Air University
AWACS	Airborne Warning and Control System
AWL	above water level
BAQ	basic aircraft qualification
BAT	biological augmentation team
BCD	battlefield coordination detachment
BCE	base civil engineer
BDA	battle damage assessment
BDC	blood donor center
BDI	battle damage indications
BEE	bioenvironmental engineer
BEMRT	basic expeditionary medical readiness training
BFT	blue force tracking
BII	base information infrastructure
BMC	basic mission capable
BMC2	battle management, command and control
BOS-I	base operations support-integration
BPC	building partnership capacity

C-CBRN	counter-chemical, biological, radiological, and nuclear
C-CBRNE	counter-chemical, biological, radiological, nuclear and high-yield explosives
C2	command and control
C2W	command and control warfare
CA	campaign assessment
CAA	combat aviation advisors
CAAT	combat aviation advisory team
CAF	combat air forces
CALFEX	combined arms live fire exercise
CAOC	combined air operations center
CAP	combat air patrol, crisis action planning, Civil Air Patrol,
CAS	close air support
CASEVAC	casualty evacuation
CAT	combat aircrew training, crisis action team
CAWG	combined assessment working group
CBRN	chemical, biological, radiological, and nuclear
CBRNE	chemical, biological, radiological, nuclear, and high yield explosives
CBU	cluster bomb unit
CC	commander
CCATT	critical care air transport team
CCD	camouflage, concealment, and deception
CCDR	combatant commander
CCIR	commander's critical intelligence requirement
CCM	contagious casualty management
CCO	contingency contracting officer
CD	collateral damage
CDM	collateral damage methodology
CDR	commander
CDRUSCENTCOM	Commander, United States Central Command
CDRUSEUCOM	Commander, United States European Command
CDRUSJFCOM	Commander, United States Joint Forces Command
CDRUSPACOM	Commander, United States Pacific Command

CDRUSSTRATCOM	Commander, United States Strategic Command
CDRUSTRANSCOM	Commander, United States Transportation Command
CDTQT	chemical defense task qualification training
CE	civil engineer
CEA	career enlisted aviator
CERT	computer emergency response team
CETS	civilian engineering technical survey
CFACC	combined force air component commander
CFC	combined force commander
CFE	commercial and foreign entities
CFT	cockpit familiarization trainer
CG	center of gravity
CHAT	chemically hardened air transportable hospital
CHUM	chart-updating manual
CI	counterintelligence
CIA	Central Intelligence Agency
CIB	combined integration board
CIC	central integrated checkout
CID	combat identification
CISR	chief of intelligence, surveillance, and reconnaissance
CJCS	Chairman, Joint Chiefs of Staff
CJCSI	Chairman, Joint Chiefs of Staff instruction
CM	consequence management
CMA	collection management authority
CMO	civil-military operations
CMSA	cruise missile support agency
CMT	combat mission training
CNA	computer network attack
COA	course of action
COCOM	combatant command (command authority)
COD	combat operations division
COG	center of gravity, continuity of government

COIN	counterinsurgency
COM	collection operations management
COMAFFOR	commander, Air Force forces
COMAFSOF	Commander Air Force Special Operations Forces
COMINT	communications intelligence
COMSPACEAF	Commander, Space Air Force Forces
CONOPS	concept of operations
CONPLAN	contingency plan
CONUS	continental United States
COOP	continuity of operations
COP	common operating picture
COS	chief of staff
COT	commissioned officer training
CPD	combat plans division
CR	combat recovery
CRAF	Civil Reserve Air Fleet
CRC	control and reporting center
CRE	contingency response element
CRG	contingency response group
CRL	container ramp load
CRM	collection requirements management
CRS	contingency response squadron
CSAF	Chief of Staff, United States Air Force
CSAR	combat search and rescue
CSC2	combat support command and control
CSS	communications systems support
CT	counterterrorism
CTO	counter threat operations
CTS	course training standards
DACT	dissimilar air combat training
DAO	defense attaché office
DATCALS	Deployable Air Traffic Control and Landing System

DCA	defensive counterair
DCGS	distributed common ground system
DCO	defense coordinating officer
DCS	defensive counterspace
DDOC	deployment distribution operations center
DE	developmental education
DEPORD	deployment order
DEWD	digital electronic warfare display
DFC	Defense force commander
DGS	distributed ground station
DH	decision height
DHS	Department of Homeland Security
DIA	Defense Intelligence Agency
DII	defense information infrastructure
DIME	diplomatic, informational, military, and economic
DIRLAUTH	direct liaison authorized
DIRMOBFOR	director of air mobility forces
DIRSPACEFOR	director of space forces
DISA	Defense Information Systems Agency
DISN	Defense Information Systems Network
DIW	defensive information warfare
DMC	deployed medical commander
DMSP	Defense Meteorological Satellite Program
DNI	Directorate of National Intelligence
DOD	Department of Defense
DOMS	Director of Military Support
DOS	Department of State
DP	personnel office symbol
DPI	desired point of impact
DRU	direct reporting unit
DSCA	defense support of civil authorities
DSO	direct support operator

DSP	Defense Support Program
DSS	decision support system
DST	decision support tools
DTRA	Defense Threat Reduction Agency
DTS	Defense Transportation System
DZ	drop zone
EAES	expeditionary aeromedical evacuation squadron
EAP	emergency actions procedures
EAS	expeditionary airlift squadron
EBAO	effects-based approach to operations
EBO	effects-based operations
EBS	expeditionary bomber squadron
ECATT	expeditionary critical air transport team
ECF	expeditionary contracting flight
ECHS	enhanced cargo handling system
ECL	engine condition lever
ECM	electronic counter measures
ECS	expeditionary combat support, electronic communication systems
EDA	estimated damage assessment
EEI	essential elements of information
EFS	expeditionary fighter squadron
EGBU	enhanced guided bomb unit
ELINT	electronic intelligence
EMCON	emissions control
EMEDS	expeditionary medical support
EML	expeditionary medical logistics
EMRC	Expeditionary Medical Readiness Course
EMS	electromagnetic spectrum
EMTF	expeditionary mobility task force
EOB	electronic order of battle
EOC	expeditionary operations center
EOD	explosive ordnance disposal

EP	emergency procedures
EPE	emergency procedures evaluation
EPLO	emergency preparedness liaison officer
EPW	enemy prisoner of war
ERCC	engine running crew change
ERD	evaluation reference date
ES	electronic warfare support
ESA	emergency safe altitude
ESP	expeditionary site planning
ESSP	expeditionary site survey process
ETA	estimated time of arrival
ETE	estimated time en-route
ETSS	extended training service specialists
EW	electronic warfare
EW Ops	electronic warfare operations
EWCC	electronic warfare coordination cell
EWR	early warning receiver
EXORD	execution order
F2T2EA	find, fix, track, target, engage, assess
FA	functional assessment
FAA	Federal Aviation Administration
FAC (A)	forward air controller (airborne)
FACC	Family Assistance Control Center
FAF	final approach fix
FAP	Family Advocacy Program
FCF	functional check flight
FCIF	flight crew information file
FCO	federal coordinating officer
FDP	flight duty period
FDS	foundational doctrine statement
FE	flight engineer
FEF	flight evaluation folder

FEMA	Federal Emergency Management Agency
FEMS	Federal Emergency Medical System
FHA	foreign humanitarian assistance
FID	foreign internal defense
FISA	Foreign Intelligence Surveillance Act
FISINT	foreign instrumentation signal intelligence
FMF	foreign military financing
FMS	foreign military sales
FOA	field operating agency
FOB	forward operating base
FP	force protection
FPI	Force protection intelligence
FPCON	force protection condition
FRAGO	fragmentary order
FRIES	fast rope insertion and extraction system
FSCM	fire support coordination measure
FSO	flight systems officer
FUNCPLAN	functional plan
FWA	fraud, waste, and abuse
GAMSS	global air mobility support system
GARS	Global Area Reference System
GAT	guidance, apportionment, and targeting (now called TET)
GBU	guided bomb unit
GCC	Global Cryptologic Center
GCCS	Global Command and Control System
GCWD	ground chemical warfare defense
GE	Global Engagement
GEO	geosynchronous earth orbit
GEODSS	Ground Based Electro-Optical Deep Space Surveillance
GEOINT	geospatial intelligence
GIG	global information grid
GMI	general military intelligence

GPS	Global Positioning System
GPS/INS	global positioning system/internal navigation system
GT	ground training
GTN	Global Transportation Network
GVR	ground hover reference
GWOT	Global War on Terrorism
HAA	height above airfield
HAT	height above threshold
HC	Chaplain Service office symbol
HCA	head of contracting authority
HD	homeland defense
HDD	heads down display
HEEDS	helicopter emergency egress device
HEELS	helicopter emergency exit lighting system
HEO	highly elliptical orbit
HLS	homeland security
HN	host nation
HP	health promotions
HPS/E	human performance, sustainment, and enhancement
HQ	headquarters
HS	homeland security
HSA	Homeland Security Act
HUMINT	human intelligence
I&W	indications and warning
IA	information attack
IADS	integrated air defense system
ICBM	intercontinental ballistic missile
ICE	integrated control enablers
IDAD	internal defense and development
IDAS/MATT	interactive defense avionics system/multi-mission advanced tactical terminal
IDMT	independent duty medical technician
IDT	infectious disease team

IFDO	Informational Flexible Deterrent Options
IHS	international health specialist
IIMC	inadvertent instrument meteorological conditions
IM	information management
IMA	individual mobility augmentee
IMINT	imagery intelligence
INFLTREP	inflight report
INMARSAT	international maritime satellite
INTELSAT	International Telecommunications Satellite Organization
INTSUM	intelligence summary
IO	information operations, influence operations
IPB	intelligence preparation of the battlefield
IPC	instructor preparatory course
IPE	individual protective equipment
IPOE	intelligence preparation of the operational environment
IQT	initial qualification training
IRBM	intermediate range ballistic missile
IRM	information resource management
ISD	Instructional System Development
ISR	intelligence, surveillance, and reconnaissance
IST	integrated skills training
ISvs	information services
IT	information technology
ITUD	integral tanker unit deployment
IW	irregular warfare
IWF	information warfare flight
IWO	information warfare organization
IWST	information warfare support team
JA	judge advocate
JA/ATT	joint airborne/air transportability training
JAC	joint analysis center
JACCE	joint air component coordination element

JAEP	joint air estimate process
JAG	Judge Advocate General at HQ USAF
JAOC	joint air operations center
JAOP	joint air operations plan
JARN	joint air request net
JAWG	joint assessment working group
JCMB	joint collection management board
JCS	Joint Chiefs of Staff
JDAM	joint direct attack munition
JDPI	joint designated point of impact
JET	joint expeditionary tasking
JEWG	joint effects working group
JFACC	joint force air component commander
JFC	joint force commander
JFCC	Space Joint Functional Component Command Space
JFO	joint fires observer
JFSOCC	joint force special operations component commander
JIATF	joint interagency task force
JIB	joint integration board
JIC	joint information center
JIIM	joint, interagency, intergovernmental, and multinational
JIOC	joint intelligence operations center
JIPCL	joint integrated prioritized collection list
JIPOE	joint intelligence preparation of the operational environment
JIPTL	joint integrated prioritized target list
JIT	just in time
JMEM	joint munitions effectiveness manual
JOA	joint operations area
JOC	joint operations center
JOPES	Joint Operations Planning and Execution System
JP	joint publication
JPOTF	joint psychological operations task force

JPRC	Joint Personnel Recovery Center
JRMPO	joint regional medical planning office
JSAT	joint security assistance training
JSCP	Joint Strategic Capabilities Plan
JSEAD	joint suppression of enemy air defense
JSOACC	joint special operations air component commander
JSOCC	joint special operations component commander
JSOP	joint space operations plan
JSOTF	joint special operations task force
JSpOC	joint space operations center
JSTARS	Joint Surveillance and Target Attack Radar System
JTA-AF	Joint Technical Architecture - Air Force
JTAC	joint terminal attack controller
JTAGS	joint tactical ground station
JTCB	joint targeting coordination board
JTCG/ME	Joint Technical Coordinating Committee for Munitions Effectiveness
JTF	joint task force
JTFEX	joint task force exercise
JTL	joint target list
JTS	Joint Training System
JWAC	Joint Warfare Analysis Center
LAF	line of the Air Force
LD/HD	low density/high demand
LEO	low Earth orbit
LFA	lead federal agency
LM	loadmaster
LNO	liaison officer
LOAC	law of armed conflict
LOC	localizer
LTT	logistics team training
LVA	low visibility approach
MAAP	master air attack plan

MACA	military assistance to civil authorities
MACDIS	military assistance for civil disturbances
MAJCOM	major command
MANPAD	man portable air defense system
MAPE	monitor, assess, plan, and execute
MARCS	media and routing control system
MASINT	measurement and signature intelligence
MCA	military civic action
MCC	medical control center
MCS	modular control system
MD	military deception
MDA	minimum descent altitude
MEA	munitions effects assessment
MEO	medium earth orbit
MET	mission essential task
MFST	mobile field surgical team
MILDEC	military deception
MISREP	mission report
Mk	Mark (general purpose bomb)
MLMC	Medical Logistics Management Center
MOE	measure of effectiveness
MoM	measure of merit
MOP	measure of performance
MOPP	mission-oriented protective posture
MPF	military personnel flight
MQF	master question file
MQT	mission qualification training
MR	mission ready
MRBM	medium-range ballistic missile
MSA	minimum safe altitude
MSCLEA	military support to civilian law enforcement agencies
MSDP	mission system data package

MSL	mean sea level
MSN	mission
MSO	mission systems officer
MSP	master space plan
MTF	medical treatment facility
MTI	moving target indicator
multi-INT	multiple intelligence
NA	national assessment
NAF	numbered air force
NAR	non-conventional assisted recovery
NASA	National Aeronautics and Space Administration
NATO	North Atlantic Treaty Organization
NCC	network control center
NCC-D	network control center -- deployed
NDP	national disclosure policy
NEAF	numbered expeditionary air force
NEO	noncombatant evacuation operation
NetA	network attack
NetD	network defense
NETOPS	network operations
NGA	National Geospatial Intelligence Agency
NGO	nongovernmental organization
NIST	national intelligence support team
NMS	National Military Strategy
NMS-CWMD	National Military Strategy to Combat Weapons of Mass Destruction
NOAA	National Oceanic and Atmospheric Administration
NORAD	North American Aerospace Defense Command
NOSC	network operations and security center
NOSC-D	network operations and security center (deployable)
NRO	National Reconnaissance Office
NRF	National Response Framework
NS	network warfare support

NSA	National Security Agency
NSL	no-strike list
NSSE	national special security event
NTISR	non-traditional intelligence surveillance and reconnaissance
NW Ops	network warfare operations
NWO	night water operations
OA	operational assessment
OAT	operational assessment team
OB	order of battle
OBIGS	onboard inert gas generating system
OBOGS	onboard oxygen generating system
OCA	offensive counterair
OCONUS	outside the continental United States
OCS	offensive counterspace
ODF	Operation DELIBERATE FORCE
OE	operational environment
OEF	Operation ENDURING FREEDOM
OFT	operational flight trainer
OGE	out off ground effect
OIF	Operation IRAQI FREEDOM
OIW	offensive information warfare
ONIR	overhead non-imaging infrared
OODA	observe, orient, decide, act
OOS	on-orbit servicing
OPCON	operational control
OPLAN	operation plan
OPORD	operation order
OPR	office of primary responsibility
OPSEC	operations security
ORI	operational readiness inspection
ORM	operational risk management
OSA	operational support airlift

OSINT	open-source intelligence
OST	Outer Space Treaty
PA	public affairs
PACAF	Pacific Air Forces
PAM	preventive aerospace medicine
PARA	policy analysis resource allocation
PBA	predictive battlespace awareness
PCA	Posse Comitatus Act
PCE	professional continuing education
PCM	primary care management
PD	passive defense
PDA	physical damage assessment
PEC	pre-authorized engagement criteria
PED	processing, exploitation, and dissemination
PERSCO	personnel support for contingency operations
PFA	primary federal agency
PFO	principal federal official
PFPS	portable flight planning software
PIR	priority intelligence requirements
PLANORD	planning order
PMESII	political, military, economic, social, infrastructure and informational
PN	partner nation
PNP	precision navigation and positioning
PNT	positioning, navigation, and timing
POL	petroleum, oil, and lubricants
POM	program objective memorandum
POTUS	President of the United States
POW	prisoner of war
PPE	personal protective equipment
PR	personnel recovery
PSI	proliferation security initiative
PSYOP	psychological operations

PTT	part task trainer
PV	prevailing visibility
PVO	private voluntary organization
QUAL	qualification
RAMCC	regional air movement control center
RC	radio combat
RED HORSE	Rapid Engineer Deployable Heavy Operational Repair Squadron, Engineer
RFA	request for federal assistance
RFI	request for information
RNP	required navigation performance
ROE	rules of engagement
ROI	reports of investigation
ROMO	range of military operations
ROVER	remote operations video enhanced receiver
RPA	remotely piloted aircraft
RPI	rated position indicator
RPL	required proficiency level
RPV	remotely piloted vehicle
RSO&I	reception, staging, on-ward movement, and integration
RSP	readiness spares packages
RSS	regional supply squadron
RSTA	reconnaissance, surveillance, and target acquisition
RSVP	Readiness Skills Verification Program
RTL	restricted target list
S&TI	scientific and technical intelligence
SA	security assistance, strategic attack
SAA	Senior Airfield Authority
SAAM	special assignment airlift mission
SACC	suppression of adversary counterspace capabilities
SADL	situation awareness data link
SAM	surface-to-air-missile
SAR	search and rescue, synthetic aperture radar

SARDO	search and rescue duty officer
SATB	standard airdrop training bundle
SATCOM	satellite communications
SBIRS	Space-based Infrared System
SC	space control, strategic communication
SCA	space coordinating authority, self-contained approach
SCNS	self-contained navigation system
SCUD	surface-to-surface missile system
SecDef	Secretary of Defense
SF	security forces
SFA	space force application
SFE	space force enhancement
SI	success indicator
SIGINT	signals intelligence
SINCGARS	single channel ground/air radio system
SIRFC	suite of integrated radio frequency countermeasures
SME	squadron medical element, subject matter expert
SNS	satellite navigation station
SOC	space operations center
SOD	space operations directive
SOF	special operations forces
SOFA	status of forces agreement
SOFPARS	special operations forces planning and rehearsal system
SOLE	special operations liaison element
SOLL	special operations low level
SOPE	special operations planning exercise
SOPS	space operations squadron
SORTIEALOT	sortie allotment message
SOSA	system of system analysis
SOTA	signals intelligence (SIGINT) operational tasking authority
SPEARR	small portable expeditionary aeromedical rapid response
SPIES	special patrol insertion and extraction systems

SPINS	special instructions
SRC	search and rescue center
SROE	standing rules of engagement
SS	space support
SSA	space situational awareness
SSN	space surveillance network
STAN/EVAL	standardization/evaluation
STANAG	standardization agreement (NATO)
STARS	scheduled theater airlift routes system
STO	space tasking order, short takeoff, special technical operations
SWS	space warning squadron
SYSCON	systems control
TA	tactical assessment
TACC	tanker airlift control center (also called 618 TACC)
TACON	tactical control
TACP	tactical air control party
TACS	theater air control system
TAFT	technical assessment field team
TAIP	tactical air force improvement plan
TALCE	tanker airlift control element
TAV	total asset visibility
TBMCS	Theater Battle Management Core System
TBMWMD	tactical ballistic missile weapon of mass destruction
TCPED	tasking, collecting, processing, exploitation and dissemination
TDY	temporary duty
TET	targeting effects team (formerly called GAT)
TF	Total Force
TF/TA	terrain following/terrain avoidance
TIC	toxic industrial chemicals
TIM	toxic industrial materials
TM	terrain masking
TMD	theater missile defense

TNL	target nomination list
TOD	task and objective document
TOLD	take-off and landing data
TPFDD	time-phased force and deployment data
TSA	target systems analysis
TSCP	theater security cooperation plan
TSG	theater surgeon
TST	time-sensitive targeting, time-sensitive target
TTP	tactics, techniques, and procedures
UA	unmanned aircraft
UAR	unconventional assisted recovery
UAS	unmanned aircraft system
UCAV	unmanned combat aerial vehicle
UCMJ	Uniform Code of Military Justice
UE	Operation UNIFIED ENDEAVOR
UET	underwater egress training
UPT	Undergraduate Pilot Training
UQT	unit qualification training
USAF	United States Air Force
USAFE	United States Air Forces Europe
USCENTAF	United States Central Command Air Forces
USCENTCOM	United States Central Command
USEUCOM	United States European Command
USJFCOM	United States Joint Forces Command
USNORTHCOM	United States Northern Command
USPACOM	United States Pacific Command
USSOCOM	United States Special Operations Command
USSTRATCOM	United States Strategic Command
USTRANSCOM	United States Transportation Command
UW	unconventional warfare
VDP	visual descent point
VMS	vehicle management system

WMD	weapons of mass destruction
WMDT	wartime medical decontamination team
WME	weapons of mass effect
WPT	weapons procedures trainer
WRM	war reserve materiel
WSSR	weapon system safety rule
WST	weapons system trainer
XATK	airborne alert attack
XCAS	airborne alert close air support
XDCA	airborne alert defensive counterair
XEW	airborne alert electronic warfare
XINT	airborne alert interdiction
XSAR	airborne alert search and rescue
XWW	airborne alert wild weasel

DEFINITONS

action

> The performance of an activity. An act or actions are taken in order to create a desired effect. Actions may be kinetic (physical, material) or non-kinetic (logical, behavioral). Actions are invariably tactical, usually producing tactical level direct effects. (AFDD 2)

active air defense

> Direct defensive action taken to destroy, nullify, or reduce the effectiveness of hostile air and missile threats against friendly forces and assets. It includes the use of aircraft, air defense weapons, electronic warfare, and other available weapons. (JP 1-02) [Direct defensive action taken to nullify or reduce the effectiveness of hostile air and missile threats against friendly forces and vital assets. It includes such measures as the use of aircraft, air defense weapons, weapons not used primarily in an air defense role, and electronic warfare.] [AFDD 3-01] {Words in brackets apply only to the Air Force and are offered for clarity.}

active defense

> The employment of limited offensive action and counterattacks to deny a contested area or position to the enemy. (JP 1-02) [Active defense operations attempt to intercept CBRN weapons en route to their targets.] (AFDD 3-40)

{Words in brackets apply only to the Air Force and are offered for clarity.}

active force protection

Measures to defend against or counter a perceived or actual threat and, if necessary, to deny, defeat, or destroy hostile forces in the act of targeting Air Force assets. (AFDD 3-10)

adversary

A party with whom one has a conflict, peaceful or otherwise. (AFDD 2)

agile combat support

The ability to create, protect, and sustain air and space forces across the full range of military operations. It is the foundational and crosscutting United States Air Force system of support that enables Air Force operational concepts and the capabilities that distinguish air and space power-speed, flexibility, and global perspective. Agile combat support is an Air Force Distinctive Capability. Also known as ACS. (AFDD 4-0)

air and space forces

Forces that operate within the air and space mediums. This includes forces that control or support those forces. (AFDD 2)

air and space PSYOP

Deliberate use of air and space power, in any of its lethal or nonlethal, kinetic or nonkinetic, forms to achieve a psychological balance advantageous to friendly forces and objectives. PSYOP may be used offensively or defensively depending on the commander's intent and the current situation. (AFDD 3-13)

air bridge

An air refueling operation that extends the unrefueled range of aircraft transiting from CONUS and a theater, or any two theaters. This operation reduces the number of aircraft on the ground at forward staging bases, minimizes potential en route maintenance delays, enables airlift assets to maximize their payloads, and facilitates rapid transit of combat aircraft to area of operations. (AFDD 3-17)

air expeditionary force

An organizational structure to provide Air Force forces and support on a rotational and thus relatively more predictable basis. They are composed of force packages of capabilities that provide rapid and responsive airpower. Also called AEF. (AFDD 1)

air expeditionary task force

The organizational manifestation of Air Force forces afield. The AETF provides a joint force commander with a task-organized, integrated package with the appropriate balance of force, sustainment, control, and force protection. Also called AETF. (AFDD 1)

Air Force Emergency Management Program

The single, integrated Air Force program to coordinate and organize efforts to manage, prepare for, respond to and recover from the direct and indirect consequences of CBRN and conventional weapon attacks, major accidents and natural disasters. The primary missions of the emergency management program are to save lives, minimize the loss or degradation of resources and continue, sustain, and restore combat and combat support operational capability in an "all hazards" physical threat environment at Air Force installations worldwide. The ancillary missions of the program are to support homeland security operations and to provide support to civil and host-nation authorities in accordance with DOD directives and through the appropriate combatant command. The program is managed by the Office of The Civil Engineer, AF/A7C. (AFDD 3-40)

air force network operations

The operation and defense of the communications system supporting the Air Force's provisioned portion of the Global Information Grid. Also called AFNETOPS. (AFDD 6-0)

air interdiction

Air operations conducted to destroy, neutralize, or delay the enemy's military potential before it can be brought to bear effectively against friendly forces at such distance from friendly forces that detailed integration of each air mission with the fire and movement of friendly forces is not required. (JP 1-02) [Includes both lethal and nonlethal systems, is employed to destroy, disrupt, divert, or delay the enemy's surface military potential before it can effectively engage friendly forces, or otherwise achieve its objectives.] [AFDD 3-01] {Words in brackets apply only to the Air Force and are offered for clarity.}

air mobility control team

A cell within the air operations center and one of the core teams in the air mobility division. The air mobility control team is the centralized source of air mobility command, control, and communications for the director of mobility forces during mission execution. The director of mobility forces uses the air mobility control team to direct (or redirect as required) air mobility forces in concert with other air and space forces to respond to requirement changes, higher priorities, or immediate execution limitations. The air mobility control team deconflicts all air mobility operations into, out of, and within the area of responsibility or joint operations area. The air mobility control team maintains execution process and communications connectivity for tasking, coordination, and flight with the air operations center's combat operations division, subordinate air mobility units, and mission forces. Also called AMCT. (AFDD 3-17)

air operations center

The senior agency of the Air Force component commander that provides command and control of Air Force air and space operations and coordinates with other components and Services. Also called AOC. (AFDD 2)

Air Reserve Component

The forces of Air National Guard and the Air Force Reserve Command. Also called ARC. (HQ AFRC, HQ ANG)

air-launched cruise missile

An air-launched vehicle designed to deliver a nuclear warhead in an air-to-ground mission. Also called ALCM. (AFDD 3-01)

airbase defense

Those measures taken to nullify or reduce the effectiveness of enemy attacks on, or sabotage of, airbases to ensure the senior commander retains the capability to accomplish assigned missions. (AFDD 3-10)

airborne mission coordinator

The coordinator who serves as an extension of the executing component's personnel recovery coordination cell (PRCC) and coordinates the recovery effort between the combat search and rescue task force (CSARTF) and the PRCC (or joint personnel recovery center) by monitoring the status of all CSARTF elements, requesting additional assets when needed, and ensuring the recovery and supporting forces arrive at their designated areas to accomplish the PR mission. The component PRCC or higher authority may designate the AMC. The AMC appoints, as necessary, an on-scene commander. Also called AMC. (AFDD 3-17)

airlift

Operations to transport and deliver forces and materiel through the air in support of strategic, operational, or tactical objectives. (AFDD 3-17)

airpower

Airpower is the ability to protect military power or influence through the control and exploitation of air, space, and cyberspace to achieve strategic, operational, or tactical objectives. (AFDD 1)

allocation (air)

The translation of the air apportionment decision into total numbers of sorties by aircraft type available for each operation or task. See also allocation. (JP 1-02) [The translation of the air apportionment decision into total numbers of sorties or missions by weapon system type available for each operation or task] [AFDD 3-1] {Italicized words in brackets apply only to the Air Force and are offered for clarity.}

assessment

1. Analysis of the security, effectiveness, and potential of an existing or planned intelligence activity. (JP 1-02) [The evaluation of progress toward the creation of effects and the achievement of objectives and end state conditions.] [AFDD 2] {Words in brackets apply only to the Air Force and are offered for clarity.}

asymmetric

Any capability that confers an advantage an adversary cannot directly compensate for. (AFDD 2)

asymmetric operations

Operations that confer disproportionate advantage on those conducting them by using capabilities the adversary cannot use, will not use, or cannot effectively defend against. (AFDD 2)

base security zone

The battlespace from which the enemy can launch an attack against base personnel and resources or aircraft approaching/departing the base. Also called BSZ. (AFDD 3-10)

battle rhythm

A commander's pace, pattern, or systematic process used to plan and execute an engagement, battle, or campaign. (AFDD 3-60)

behavioral effect

An effect on the behavior of individuals, groups, systems, organizations, and governments. (AFDD 2)

blue force tracking

The employment of techniques to identify US, allied, and coalition forces for the purposes of providing commanders enhanced situational awareness and reducing fratricide. Also called BFT. (AFDD 3-60)

campaign assessment

The joint force commander's broad qualitative and analytical determination of the overall campaign progress, effectiveness of operations and recommendations for future action. Also called CA. (AFDD 2)

cascading effect

One or more of a series of successive indirect effects that propagate through a system or systems. Typically, cascading effects flow throughout the levels of conflict and are the results of interdependencies and links among multiple connected systems. (AFDD 2)

causal linkage

An explanation of why an action or effect will cause or contribute to a given effect. (AFDD 2)

center of gravity

The source of power that provides moral or physical strength, freedom of action, or will to act. Also called COG. (JP 1-02) [In the context of strategic attack against enemy systems, COGs are focal points that hold a system or structure together and draw power from a variety of sources and provide purpose and direction to that system.] [AFDD 3-70] {The statement in brackets applies only to the Air Force and is offered for clarity.}

centralized control

In joint air operations, placing within one commander the responsibility and authority for planning, directing, and coordinating a military operation or group/category of operations. (JP 1-02) [The planning, direction, prioritization, allocation, synchronization, integration, and deconfliction of air, space and cyberspace capabilities to achieve the objectives of the joint force commander.] (AFDD 1) {Words in brackets apply only to the Air Force and are offered for clarity.}

chemical agent

Any toxic chemical intended for use in military operations. (JP 1-02) [A chemical substance which is intended for use in military operations to kill, seriously injure, or incapacitate personnel through its physiological effects. The term excludes riot control agents, herbicides, smoke, and flame.] [AFDD 3-40] {Words in brackets apply only to the Air Force and are offered for clarity.}

civil environment

The civil environment includes factors related to a people, their government, politics, culture, and economy. The organization of the civil environment includes the major subcategories of political policies, culture, and economy. (AFDD 1-1)

Civil Reserve Air Fleet

A voluntary contractual program where civil carriers agree to augment military airlift during a crisis in exchange for peacetime defense business. During peacetime, regional contingencies, and major exercises, CRAF carriers are contracted to fly scheduled passenger, patient/casualty, and cargo channel missions, special assignment airlift missions (SAAMs) and charter missions. This support gives AMC the capacity to meet both routine scheduled and surge commitments flexibly and simultaneously. Also called CRAF. (AFDD 3-17)

coalition force

A force composed of military elements of nations that have formed a temporary alliance for some specific purpose. (AFDD 3-05)

coercion

Persuading an adversary to behave differently than it otherwise would through the threat or use of force. (AFDD 2)

combat aviation advisory team

A special operations team specifically tailored to assess, advise, and train foreign aviation forces in air operations employment and sustainability. Teams support geographic combatant commanders throughout the operational continuum, primarily by facilitating the integration and interoperability of friendly and allied aviation forces supporting joint and multinational operations. Teams are specially trained and equipped to provide advisory assistance in the three interrelated areas of foreign internal defense (FID), coalition support (CS), and unconventional warfare (UW). Also called CAAT. (AFDD 3-05)

combat identification

The capability to attain an accurate characterization of detected objects in the joint battlespace to the extent that high confidence, timely application of military options and weapons resources can occur. Depending on the situation and the operational decisions that must be made, this characterization may be limited to "enemy," "friend," or "neutral." In other situations, other characterizations may be required—including, but not limited to class, type, nationality, mission configuration, status, and intent. Also call CID. (AFDD 3-60)

combat offload

An expeditious procedure for offloading cargo while an aircraft is taxiing, to reduce the ground time and materials handling equipment at an air terminal. This procedure is potentially more hazardous due to the dynamic nature of the operation. (AFDD 3-60)

combat recovery

The act of retrieving resources while engaging enemy forces. (AFDD 3-05)

combat search and rescue

Combat search and rescue is how the Air Force accomplishes the personnel recovery task. It is the Air Force's preferred mechanism for personnel recovery execution in uncertain or hostile environments and denied areas. Also called CSAR. (AFDD 3-50)

combat support

Fire support and operational assistance provided to combat elements. Also called CS. (JP 1-02) [Provides the foundation for and is the enabler of the Air Force distinctive capabilities. It includes the actions taken to ready, sustain, and protect personnel, assets, and capabilities through all peacetime and wartime military operations. Furthermore, it supports the unique contributions of air and space power: speed, flexibility, versatility, and global reach.] [AFDD 4-0] {Italicized words in brackets apply only to the Air Force and are offered for clarity.}

commander Air Force special operations forces

The senior AFSOF Airman on the JFSOC or JSOTF chain of command. Also called COMAFSOF. (AFDD 3-05)

commander, Air Force Forces

The senior US Air Force officer designated as commander of the US Air Force component assigned to a joint force commander (JFC) at the unified, subunified, and joint task force level. In this position, the COMAFFOR presents the single US Air Force voice to the JFC. Also called COMAFFOR. (AFDDs 1, 2)

computer network attack

Operations to disrupt, deny, degrade, or destroy information resident in computers and computer networks, or the computers and networks themselves. Electronic attack (EA) can be used against a computer, but it is not computer network attack (CNA). CNA relies on the data stream to execute the attack while EA relies on the electromagnetic spectrum. An example of the two operations is the following: sending a code or instruction to a central processing unit that causes the computer to short out the power supply is CNA. Using an electromagnetic pulse device to destroy a computer's electronics and causing the same result is EA. (AFDD 3-13)

consequence management

Actions taken to maintain or restore essential services and manage and mitigate problems resulting from disasters and catastrophes, including natural, manmade, or terrorist incidents. Also called CM. (JP 1-02) [CM activities serve to reduce the effects of a CBRN attack or event and assist in the restoration of essential operations and services at home and abroad in a permissive environment.] [AFDD 3-40] {Words in brackets apply only to the Air Force and are offered for clarity.}

continuum of learning

A career-long process of individual development where challenging experiences are combined with education and training through a common taxonomy to produce Airmen who possess the tactical expertise, operational competence, and strategic vision to lead and execute the full spectrum of Air Force missions. (AFDD 1-1)

coordination

The necessary action to ensure adequate exchange of information to integrate, synchronize, and deconflict operations between separate organizations. Coordination is not necessarily a process of gaining approval but is most often used for mutual exchange of information. Normally used between functions of a supporting staff. Direct liaison authorized (DIRLAUTH) is used to coordinate with an organization outside of the immediate staff or organization. (AFDD 1)

core task

A task adapted from the Air Force core competencies or their command and control. (AFDD 6-0)

core values

A statement of those institutional values and principles of conduct that provide the moral framework within which military activities take place. The professional Air Force ethic consists of three fundamental and enduring values of integrity, service before self, and excellence in all we do. (AFDD 1-1)

coronet

Movements of air assets, usually fighter aircraft, in support of contingencies, rotations, exercises, or aircraft movements for logistics purposes. (AFDD 3-17)

counter threat operations

The Air Force Office of Special Investigations 'capability to find, fix, track, and neutralize the enemy in order to create a sustained permissive environment for military forces, as well as provide a safe and secure operating environment. Also called CTO. (AFDD 3-24, AFMD 39)

counter-chemical, biological, radiological, and nuclear

Activities taken to detect, deter, disrupt, deny, or destroy an adversary's CBRN capabilities and to minimize the effects of an enemy CBRN attack. Note: The interlinked components of C-CBRN operations are proliferation prevention, counterforce, active defense, passive defense, and consequence management. Also called C-CBRN. (AFDD 3-40)

counterair

A mission that integrates offensive and defensive operations to attain and maintain a desired degree of air superiority. Counterair missions are designed to destroy or negate enemy aircraft and missiles, both before and after launch. (JP 1-02) [Counterair integrates and exploits the mutually beneficial effects of offensive and defensive operations by fixed- and rotary-wing aircraft, surface-to-air and air-to-air missiles, antiaircraft guns, artillery, and electronic warfare to destroy or neutralize enemy aircraft and missile forces both before and after launch.] [AFDD 3-01] {Words in brackets apply only to the Air Force and are offered for clarity.}

counterforce

The employment of strategic air and missile forces in an effort to destroy, or render impotent, selected military capabilities of an enemy force under any of the circumstances by which hostilities may be initiated. (JP 1-02)[Counterforce operations aim to detect, deter, deny, degrade, or destroy adversary CBRN capabilities including research and development, production, and storage facilities, fielded forces, and related C2.] (AFDD 3-40) {Words in brackets apply only to the Air Force and are offered for clarity.}

counterland

Operations conducted to attain and maintain a desired degree of superiority over surface operations by the destruction, disrupting, delaying, diverting, or other neutralization of enemy forces. The main objectives of counterland operations are to dominate the surface environment and prevent the opponent from doing the same. (AFDD 3-03)

counterproliferation

Counterproliferation refers to the activities of the full range of US efforts to combat proliferation, including diplomacy, arms control, export controls, and intelligence collection and analyses, with particular responsibility for assuring that US forces and interests can be protected should they confront an adversary armed with weapons of mass destruction or missiles. (AFDD 3-40)

counterpropaganda operations

Those psychological operations activities that identify adversary propaganda, contribute to situational awareness, and serve to expose adversary attempts to influence friendly populations and military forces. (JP 1-02) [Activities to identify and counter adversary propaganda and expose adversary attempts to influence friendly populations and military forces situational understanding.] [AFDD 3-13] {Words in brackets apply only to the Air Force and are offered for clarity.}

countersea

Operations conducted to attain and maintain a desired degree of superiority over maritime operations by the destruction, disrupting, delaying, diverting, or other neutralization of enemy naval forces. The main objectives of countersea operations are to dominate the maritime environment and prevent the opponent from doing the same. (AFDD 3-04)

counterspace

Those offensive and defensive operations conducted by air, land, sea, space, special operations, and information forces with the objective of gaining and maintaining control of activities conducted in or through the space environment. (AFDD 3-14)

counterthreat operations

The AFOSI's capability to find, fix, track, and neutralize enemy threats in order to create a sustained permissive environment for air, space, and cyberspace operations. Also called CTO. (AFDD 3-10)

critical vulnerabilities

Vulnerable components, conditions, or resources of a COG vital to its operation, and susceptible to moral or physical attack that will achieve the most decisive effects in neutralization, degradation, or destruction of the centers of gravity. (AFDD 3-70)

cumulative effect

An effect resulting from the aggregation of multiple, contributory direct or indirect effects. (AFDD 2)

cyberspace

Cyberspace is a global domain within the information environment consisting of the interdependent network of information technology infrastructures, including the Internet, telecommunications networks, computer systems, and embedded processors and controllers. (JP1-02) [Cyberspace is a domain that requires man-made technology to enter and exploit. The only difference is that it is easier to see and sense the other domains. As with air and space, effects of cyberspace operations can occur simultaneously in many places. They can be precise, broad, enduring, and transitory.] {Definition in brackets applies only to the Air Force and is offered for clarity.} (AFDD 3-12)

decentralized execution

Delegation of execution authority to subordinate commanders. (JP 1-02) [Decentralized execution of air power is the delegation of execution authority to responsible and capable lower-level commanders to achieve effective span of control and to foster disciplined initiative, situational responsiveness, and tactical flexibility.] [AFDD 1] {Words in brackets apply only to the Air Force and are offered for clarity.}

decision superiority

A competitive advantage, enabled by an ongoing situational awareness that allows commanders and their forces to make better-informed decisions and implement them faster than their adversaries can react. (AFDD 3-13)

decision support systems/tools

A compilation of processes and systems developed from the application of maturing information systems technologies that provide the warfighter and the logistician with the means to rapidly plan, execute, monitor, and replan logistical operations in a collaborative environment that is responsive to operational requirements. (AFDD 4-0)

defense force commander

The senior Air Force commander responsible for the air base normally delegates operational authority to conduct integrated base defense to the defense force commander. The defense force commander exercises command and control through an established chain of command and directs the planning and execution of base defense operations. Also called DFC. (AFDD 3-10)

defensive counterair

All defensive measures designed to detect, identify, intercept, and destroy or negate enemy forces attempting to attack or penetrate the friendly air environment. Also called DCA. See also counterair; offensive counterair. (JP 1-02) [Defensive counterair operations are synonymous with air defense operations. Defensive counterair encompasses both active and passive measures and is normally conducted near or over friendly territory and generally reacts to the initiative of enemy forces.] [AFDD 3-01] {Words in brackets apply only to the Air Force and are offered for clarity.}

defensive counterspace

Operations to preserve US/friendly ability to exploit space to its advantage via active and passive actions to protect friendly space-related capabilities from adversary attack or interference. Also called DCS. (AFDD 3-01)

deliberate targeting

The part of the tasking process for prosecuting targets that are detected, identified, and developed in sufficient time to schedule actions against them in tasking cycle products such as the air tasking order. (AFDD 3-60)

deliverables

The desired or expected results of specific support functions that contribute to responsive combat support for an air and space expeditionary force. (AFDD 4-0)

denial

A form of coercion strategy that destroys or neutralizes a portion of the adversary's physical means to resist. (AFDD 2)

direct effect

First-order result of an action with no intervening effect between action and outcome. Usually immediate, physical, and readily recognizable (e.g., weapons employment results). (AFDD 2)

direction

Guidance to or management of support staff functions. Inherent within command but not a command authority in its own right. In some cases, can be considered an explicit instruction or order. Used by commanders and their designated subordinates to facilitate, channel, or motivate support staff to achieve appropriate action, tempo, or intensity. Used by directors of staff agencies on behalf of the commander to provide guidance to their staffs on how best to accomplish stated objectives IAW the commander's intent. (AFDD 1)

DIRSPACEFOR

The Air Force officer serving as the senior space advisor to the commander, Air Force forces (COMAFFOR) or the COMAFFOR/joint force air and space component commander (JFACC). The DIRSPACEFOR conducts coordination, integration, and staffing activities to tailor space support for the COMAFFOR or COMAFFOR / JFACC. (AFDD 3-14)

distributed operations

The process of conducting operations from independent or interdependent nodes in a teaming manner. Some operational planning or decision-making may occur from outside the joint area of operations. The goal of a distributed operation is to support the operational commander in the field; it is not a method of command from the rear. See also split operations. (AFDD 6-0)

dynamic targeting

The part of the tasking process for prosecuting targets that are not detected, identified, or developed in time to be included in deliberate targeting, and therefore have not had actions scheduled against them. (AFDD 3-60)

education

Instruction and study focused on creative problem solving that does not provide predictable outcomes. Education encompasses a broader flow of information to the student and encourages exploration into unknown areas and creative problem solving. (AFDD 1-1)

effect

1. The physical or behavioral state of a system that results from an action, a set of actions, or another effect. 2. The result, outcome, or consequence of an action. 3. A change to a condition, behavior, or degree of freedom. (AFDD 2)

effect indicator

Independent, qualitative or quantitative condition(s) that indicates the achievement of an effect. (AFDD 3-60)

effects

A full range of outcomes, events, or consequences of a particular cause. The cause may be an action, a set of actions, or another effect. The action can derive from any element of power—economic, political, military, diplomatic, or informational—and may occur at any point across the continuum from peace to global conflict. (AFDD 3-70)

effects-based

Actions, such as operations, targeting, or strategy that are designed to produce distinctive and desired effects while avoiding unintended or undesired effects. (AFDD 3-70)

effects-based approach to operations

Operations that are planned, executed, assessed and adapted to influence or change system behavior or capabilities in order to achieve desired outcomes. Also called EBAO. (Note: Sometimes colloquially but incorrectly referred to as "effects-based operations," or EBO) (AFDD 2)

electronic warfare operations

The integrated planning, employment, and assessment of military capabilities to achieve desired effects across the electromagnetic domain in support of operational objectives. Also called EW Ops. (AFDD 3-13)

emerging target

A potential target, which, upon initial detection, meets sufficient criteria to be considered and further developed. The criticality and time sensitivity of the potential target is initially undetermined. (AFDD 3-60)

end state

The set of conditions that needs to be achieved to resolve the situation or conflict on satisfactory terms, as defined by appropriate authority. (AFDD 2)

enemy

An adversary who opposes one's will through use of force. (AFDD 2)

expeditionary combat support

A subset of agile combat support that responds quickly, is highly mobile, technologically superior, robust, flexible, and fully integrated with operations. Expeditionary combat support is the deployed agile combat support capability to provide persistent and effective support for the applications of air and space power on a global basis. Also known as ECS. (AFDD 4-0)

force development

A deliberate process of preparing Airmen through the continuum of learning with the required competencies to meet the challenges of current and future operating environments. (AFDD 1-1)

force health protection

A comprehensive threat-based program directed at preventing and managing health-related actions against Air Force uncommitted combat power. (AFDD 4-02)

force protection

Preventive measures taken to mitigate hostile actions against Department of Defense personnel (to include family members), resources, facilities, and critical information. Force protection does not include actions to defeat the enemy or protect against accidents, weather, or disease. Also called FP. (JP 1-02) [The process of detecting threats and hazards to the Air Force and its mission, and applying measures to deter, pre-empt, negate or mitigate them based on an acceptable level of risk.] (AFDD 3-10) {Italicized definition in brackets applies only to the Air Force and is offered for clarity.}

force protection intelligence

Analyzed, all-source information concerning threats to DOD missions, people, or resources arising from terrorists, criminal entities, foreign intelligence and security services and opposing military forces. Also called FPI. (AFDD 3-10)

full spectrum threat response program

The single, integrated Air Force program to address the full spectrum of physical risks, threats, mitigation strategies, and passive defense measures. The primary missions of the Air Force full spectrum threat response program are to 1) save lives, 2) minimize the loss or degradation of resources, and 3) continue, sustain, and restore combatant combat support operational capability in an "all hazards" physical threat environment at Air force installations worldwide. The ancillary missions of the full spectrum threat response program are to support Department of Defense homeland defense operations and to provide military support to civil and host nation authorities in accordance with Department of Defense directives and through the appropriate combatant command. The full spectrum threat response program is managed by the office of the Civil Engineer, HQ USAF/A7C. Also called FSTR. (AFDD 3-27)

functional effect

An effect on the ability of a system to function properly. (AFDD 2)

fusion

In intelligence usage, the process of examining all sources of intelligence and information to derive a complete assessment of activity. (JP 1-02) [Process of combining/aggregating data to derive a more complete assessment of a specific capability, action, or situation.] [AFDD 3-13] {Words in brackets apply only to the Air Force and are offered for clarity.}

garrison

A permanent Air Force base where Airmen execute and support air and space operations. Also referred to as home station. (AFDD 4-0)

geospatial intelligence

The exploitation and analysis of imagery and geospatial information to describe, assess, and visually depict physical features and geographically referenced activities on the earth. Also known as GEOINT. (AFDD 2-0)

global air mobility support system

Provides responsive, worldwide support to airlift and air refueling operations. This system consists of an existing but limited set of CONUS and en route locations. Deployable forces capable of augmenting the fixed en route locations or establishing en route locations where none exist are also an integral part of this system. Also called GAMSS. (AFDD 3-17)

homeland defense

The protection of US territory, sovereignty, domestic population, and critical infrastructure against external threats and aggression. Also called HD. (AFDD 3-27)

homeland security

A concerted national effort to prevent terrorist attack within the United States, reduce America's vulnerability to terrorism, and minimize the damage and recover from attacks that do occur. Also called HS. (AFDD 3-27)

humanitarian operation

An air mobility operation specifically mounted to alleviate human suffering where responsible civil actors in an area are unable or unwilling to adequately support a population. It may precede, parallel, or complement the activity of specialized civil humanitarian organizations. (AFDD 3-17)

indirect effect

A second, third, or nth-order effect created through an intermediate effect or causal linkage following a causal action. It may be physical, psychological, functional, or systemic in nature. It may be created in a cumulative, cascading, sequential, or parallel manner. An indirect effect is often delayed and typically is more difficult to recognize and assess than a direct effect. (AFDD 2)

indirect support

Security assistance and other efforts to develop and sustain host nation capabilities. This definition establishes a distinction between security assistance and forms of support involving direct operational employment of US forces which supports the guidance in the National Security Strategy of the US. (AFDD 3-22)

influence operations

Employment of capabilities to affect behaviors, protect operations, communicate commander's intent, and project accurate information to achieve desired effects across the cognitive domain. These effects should result in differing behavior or a change in the adversary decision cycle, which aligns with the commander's objectives. (AFDD 3-13)

information assurance

Information operations that protect and defend information and information systems by ensuring their availability, integrity, authentication, confidentiality, and non-repudiation. This includes providing for restoration of information systems by incorporating protection, detection, and reaction capabilities. Also called IA. See also information; information operations; information system. (JP 1-02) [The Air Force prefers the DOD definition found in DODD 8500.1 "Measures that protect and defend information and information systems by ensuring their availability, integrity, authentication, confidentiality, and nonrepudiation. This includes providing for restoration of information systems by incorporating protection, detection, and reaction capabilities"] [AFDD 3-13]

{Words in brackets apply only to the Air Force and is offered for clarity.}

information attack

An activity taken to manipulate or destroy an adversary's information systems without visibly changing the physical entity within which it resides. (AFDD 3-13)

information dissemination management

The subset of information management with a supporting infrastructure that addresses awareness, access, and delivery of information. The primary mission is to provide the right information to the right person, in the right format, at the right place and time in accordance with commanders' information dissemination policies while optimizing the use of information infrastructure resources. It involves the compilation, cataloging, caching, distribution, and retrieval of data; manages the information flow to users; and enables the execution of the commanders' information dissemination policy. (AFDD 3-13)

information operations

The integrated employment, during military operations, of information-related capabilities in concert with other lines of operation to influence, disrupt, corrupt, or usurp the decision-making of adversaries and potential adversaries while protecting our own. Also called IO. (SecDef Memo 12401-10)

information protection

Policies, processes and implementation of risk management to prevent the compromise, loss, unauthorized access/disclosure, destruction, distortion or non-accessibility of information, regardless of physical form or characteristics, over the life cycle of the information. Includes actions to regulate access to sensitive information, controlled unclassified information and classified information. (AFPD 16-14)

information superiority

That degree of dominance in the information domain which permits the conduct of operations without effective opposition. (JP 1-02) Note: The Air Force prefers to cast 'superiority' as a state of relative advantage, not a capability, and views information superiority as: [the degree of dominance in the information domain which allows friendly forces the ability to collect, control, exploit, and defend information without effective opposition.] [AFDD 3-12] {Words in brackets apply only to the Air Force and is offered for clarity.}

information technology

An umbrella term describing the suite of tools used for managing and processing information. These tools can include any communications device or computer, its ancillary equipment, software applications, and related supporting resources. Also called IT. (AFDD 3-13)

institutional competencies

A measurable cluster of skills, knowledge, and abilities required of all Airmen and needed to operate successfully in a constantly changing environment. (AFDD 1-1)

Integrated Air and Missile Defense

The integration of capabilities and overlapping operations to defend the Homeland and US national interests, protect the joint force, and enable freedom of action by negating an adversary's ability to achieve adverse effects from their air and missile capabilities. (AFDD 3-52)

integrated control enablers

Critical capabilities required to execute successful air, space, and information operations and produce integrated effects for the joint fight. Includes intelligence, surveillance, and reconnaissance, network operations, and precision navigation and timing. Also called ICE. (AFDD 3-13)

integrated defense

The integration of multidisciplinary active and passive, offensive and defensive capabilities, employed to mitigate potential risks and defeat adversary threats to Air Force operations. (AFI 31-101)

intelligence fusion cell

Cell providing the base defense force with analyzed or vetted all-source information that drives effective force protection decisions and operations. (AFDD 3-10)

intelligence preparation of the operational environment

The analytical process used by intelligence organizations to produce intelligence estimates and other intelligence products in support of the joint force commander's decision-making process. It is a continuous process that includes defining the operational environment; describing the impact of the operational environment; evaluating the adversary; and determining adversary courses of action. Also called IPOE. (JP 2-01.3)

intelligence, surveillance, and reconnaissance

Integrated capabilities to collect, process, exploit and disseminate accurate and timely information that provides the battlespace awareness necessary to successfully plan and conduct operations. (AFDD 2-0)

intended effect

A proactively sought effect. (AFDD 2)

interference

Interference is any electrical disturbance that causes undesirable responses in electronic equipment. (AFDD 3-13.1)

internal development

Actions taken by a nation to promote its growth by building viable institutions (political, military, economic, and social) that respond to the needs of its society. (AFDD 3-22)

intrusion

Movement of a unit or force within another nation's specified operational area outside of territorial seas and territorial airspace for surveillance or intelligence gathering in time of peace or tension. (JP 1-02) [Intrusion is intentionally inserting electromagnetic energy into transmission paths in any manner. The object is to deceive equipment operators or cause confusion. The enemy conducts intrusion operations against us by inserting false information into our receiver paths. This false information may consist of voice instructions, ghost targets, coordinates for fire missions, or even rebroadcasting or prerecorded data transmissions.] [AFDD 3-13.1] {Words in brackets apply only to the Air Force and are offered for clarity.}

irregular warfare

A violent struggle among state and non-state actors for legitimacy and influence over the relevant populations. (JP 1, AFDD 3-24)

joint air operations center

A jointly staffed facility established for planning, directing, and executing joint air operations in support of the joint force commander's operation or campaign objectives. Also called JAOC. (JP 1-02) [Joint operational campaign planning and execution is conducted through the joint air operations center (AOC). The joint air component commander (JFACC) uses the JAOC to command and control the integrated air and space effort to meet JFC objectives.] (AFDD 2) {Words in brackets apply only to the Air Force and are offered for clarity.}

joint personnel recovery center

A primary joint personnel recovery (PR) node. The center is suitably staffed by supervisory personnel and equipped for planning, coordinating, and executing joint PR within the geographical area assigned to the joint force. The facility is operated jointly by personnel from two or more Service or functional components or it may have a multinational staff of personnel from two or more allied or coalition nations. Also called JPRC. (AFDD 3-50)

joint special operations air detachment

The JSOAD is a tactical level C2 node composed of joint aviation units that normally is subordinate to a theater JFSOCC, JSOTF, or JSOACC depending on the size and duration of the operation. (AFDD 3-05)

kill box

A three-dimensional area reference that enables timely, effective coordination and control and facilitates rapid attacks. (JP 1-02) [A generic term for a preplanned airspace control measure and/or a fire support coordination measure used by the joint force to integrate and synchronize air and surface operations and deconflict joint fires in an expedient manner or on an asymmetric battlefield.] [AFDD 3-03] {Words in brackets apply only to the Air Force and are offered for clarity.}

kinetic

Relating to actions that involve the forces and energy of moving bodies, including physical damage to or destruction of targets through use of bombs, missiles, bullets, and similar projectiles. (AFDD 3-60)

leadership

The art and science of motivating, influencing, and directing Airmen to understand and accomplish the Air Force mission. (AFDD 1-1)

link

A behavioral, physical, or functional relationship between nodes in a system. (AFDD 2)

malware

Software such as viruses or Trojans designed to cause damage or disruption to a computer system. (AFDD 3-12)

maneuver

1. A movement to place ships, aircraft, or land forces in a position of advantage over the enemy. 2. A tactical exercise carried out at sea, in the air, on the ground, or on a map in imitation of war. 3. The operation of a ship, aircraft, or vehicle, to cause it to perform desired movements. 4. Employment of forces in the battlespace through movement in combination with fires to achieve a position of advantage in respect to the enemy in order to accomplish the mission. (JP 1-02) [Air and space power is a maneuver element in its own right, co-equal with land and maritime power; as such, it is no longer merely a supporting force to surface combat. As a maneuver element, it can be supported by surface forces in attaining its assigned objectives.] [AFDD 2] {Words in brackets apply only to the Air Force and are offered for clarity.}

meaconing

A system of receiving radio beacon signals and rebroadcasting them on the same frequency to confuse navigation. The meaconing stations cause inaccurate bearings to be obtained by aircraft or ground stations. (JP 1-02) [Successful enemy meaconing causes: 1. Aircraft to be lured into hot landing zones or enemy airspace 2. Bombers to expend ordnance on false targets. 3. Ground stations to receive inaccurate bearings or position locations.] [AFDD 3-13.1] {Words in brackets apply only to the Air Force and are offered for clarity.}

measure of effect

Independent qualitative or quantitative empirical measure assigned to an intended effect, against which the effect's achievement is assessed. Also call MOE. (AFDD 2)

measure of performance

A quantitative empirical measure of achieved actions against associated planned/required actions and against which a task's or other action's accomplishment, is assessed. Also called MOP. (AFDD 2)

measures and indicators

Encompassing term for the various criteria used to evaluate progress within the assessment process (AFDD 3-60)

mission assurance (cyberspace)

Measures required to accomplish essential objectives of missions in a contested environment. Mission assurance entails prioritizing mission essential functions, mapping mission dependence on cyberspace, identifying vulnerabilities, and mitigating risk of known vulnerabilities. (AFDD 3-12)

national assessment

A broad, overarching review of the effectiveness of national security strategy and whether national leadership's objectives for a particular operation or campaign are being met. Also called NA. (AFDD 2)

network attack

The employment of network-based capabilities to destroy, disrupt, corrupt, or usurp information resident in or transiting through networks. Networks include telephony and data services networks. Also called NetA. (AFDD 3-13)

network defense

The employment of network-based capabilities to defend friendly information resident in or transiting through networks against adversary efforts to destroy, disrupt, corrupt, or usurp it. Also called NetD. (AFDD 3-13)

network management

The execution of the set of activities required for controlling, planning, allocating, deploying, coordinating, and monitoring the resources of a telecommunications network, including performing actions such as initial network planning, frequency allocation, predetermined traffic routing to support load balancing, cryptographic key distribution authorization, configuration management, fault management, security management, performance management, and accounting management. (AFDD 3-13)

network operations

The integrated planning and employment of military capabilities to provide the friendly net environment needed to plan, control and execute military operations and conduct Service functions. NetOps provides operational planning and control. It involves time-critical, operational-level decisions that direct configuration changes and information routing. Network operations risk management and command and control decisions are based on a fused assessment of intelligence, ongoing operations, commander's intent, blue and gray situation, net health, and net security. NetOps provides the three operational elements of information assurance, network/system management, and information dissemination management. Also called NetOps. (AFDD 3-13)

network warfare operations

Network warfare operations are the integrated planning and employment of military capabilities to achieve desired effects across the interconnected analog and digital portion of the battlespace. Network warfare operations are conducted in the information domain through the dynamic combination of hardware, software, data, and human interaction. Also called NW Ops. (AFDD 3-13)

network warfare support

Actions tasked by or under direct control of an operational commander to search for, intercept, identify, and locate or localize sources of access and vulnerability for the purpose of immediate threat recognition, targeting, planning, and conduct of future operations. Also called NS. (AFDD 3-13)

no-strike list

A list of geographic areas, complexes, or installations not planned for capture or destruction. Attacking these may violate the law of armed conflict or interfere with friendly relations with indigenous personnel or governments. Also called NSL. (JP 1-02) [The no-strike list is a list of geographic areas, complexes, installations, or personnel not planned for capture or destruction. Attacking personnel may violate LOAC or interfere with friendly relations with indigenous personnel or governments.] [AFDD 3-60] {Words in brackets apply only to the Air Force and are offered for clarity.}

node

A tangible entity that is a physical, functional, or behavioral element of a system. (AFDD 2)

non-kinetic

Relating to actions that produce effects without direct use of the force or energy of moving objects, including such means as electromagnetic radiation, directed energy, information operations, etc. (AFDD 3-60)

offensive counterair

Offensive operations to destroy, disrupt, or neutralize enemy aircraft, missiles, launch platforms, and their supporting structures and systems both before and after launch, but as close to their source as possible. Offensive counterair operations range throughout enemy territory and are generally conducted at the initiative of friendly forces. These operations include attack operations, fighter sweep, escort, and suppression of enemy air defenses. Also called OCA. See also counterair; defensive counterair; operation. Also called OCA. (JP 1-02) [Offensive counterair operations range throughout enemy territory and are generally conducted at the initiative of friendly forces.] [AFDD 3-01] {Words in brackets apply only to the Air Force and are offered for clarity.}

offensive counterspace.

Operations to preclude an adversary from exploiting space to their advantage. Also called OCS. (AFDD 3-14.1)

offensive force protection

Proactive measures taken to deny, defeat, or destroy hostile forces who currently are not committed to direct hostile activity but whose intent is to target Air Force assets not currently engaged in combat operations. (AFDD 3-10)

on-scene commander

The person designated to coordinate the personnel recovery efforts at the recovery site. Also called OSC. (AFDD 3-50)

OODA Loop

The process of observing phenomena, orienting mentally toward them, deciding upon a course of action concerning them, and acting on that decision. Also known as the decision cycle. (AFDD 2)

operational assessment

Joint force components' evaluation of the achievement of their objectives, both tactical and operational, through assessment of effects, operational execution, environmental influences, and attainment of the objectives' success indicators, in order to develop strategy recommendations. It also includes any required analysis of causal linkages. Also called OA. (AFDD 2)

operational risk management

The systematic process of identifying hazards, assessing risks, analyzing risk control measures, making control decisions, implementing risk controls, and supervising and reviewing the process. Commanders accept the residual risks. (AFDD 6-0)

parallel attack

Offensive military action that strikes a wide array of targets in a short period of time in order to cause maximum shock and dislocation effects across an entire enemy system. (AFDD 2)

parallel effect

The result of actions or effects that are imposed at the same time or near-simultaneously. (AFDD 2)

parallel operations

Operations that apply pressure at many points across a system in a short period of time in order to cause maximum shock and dislocation effects across that system. (AFDD 2)

passive defense

Measures taken to reduce the probability of and to minimize the effects of damage caused by hostile action without the intention of taking the initiative. (JP 1-02) [To protect US, allied, and coalition forces against NBC effects, including measures to detect and identify NBC agents, individual and collective protection equipment, NBC medical response, vaccines for BW defense, and NBC decontamination capabilities.] [AFDD 3-40] {Words in brackets apply only to the Air Force and are offered for clarity.}

passive force protection

Measures to negate or reduce the effects of hostile acts on Air Force assets by making them more survivable. This can be proactively accomplished through training, education, hardening, camouflage, concealment, deception, information security, and low/zero observable execution. (AFDD 3-10)

personal protective equipment

Personal protective equipment is equipment designed to protect individuals exposed to hazards from injury or illness in nonmilitary unique occupational environments where OSHA or applicable AFOSH standards apply, including emergency response to CBRNE incidents in the United States. Also called PPE. (AFDD 3-40)

personnel recovery

The aggregation of military, civil, and political efforts to obtain the release or recovery of personnel from uncertain or hostile environments and denied areas whether they are captured, missing, or isolated. That includes US, allied, coalition, friendly military, or paramilitary, and others as designated by the President or Secretary of Defense. Personnel recovery (PR) is the umbrella term for operations that are focused on the task of recovering captured, missing, or isolated personnel from harm's way. PR includes but is not limited to theater search and rescue; combat search and rescue; search and rescue; survival, evasion, resistance, and escape; evasion and escape; and the coordination of negotiated as well as forcible recovery options. PR can occur through military action, action by nongovernmental organizations, other US Government-approved action, and/or diplomatic initiatives, or through any of these. Also called PR. (AFDD 3-50)

personnel recovery coordination cell

A primary personnel recovery facility suitably staffed by supervisory personnel and equipped for coordinating and controlling personnel recovery operations. The facility is operated unilaterally by personnel of a single Service or jointly by functional component. For Navy component operations, this facility may be called a rescue coordination team. Also called PRCC (or RCT for Navy component). (AFDD 3-50)

Personnel Support for Contingency Operations

The collection of manual and automated procedures, systems, hardware, personnel agencies, and deployable teams to accomplish total force accountability, casualty reporting, strength reporting, and personnel program support. Total force accountability is primary mission of PERSCO—providing personnel support to the warfighter. Also called PERSCO. (AFDD 4-0)

PHOENIX RAVEN

Specially trained security forces teams that deploy with the airmobility aircraft to mitigate threats. These teams are comprised of individuals trained and equipped to provide protection of the aircraft and/or aircrews when transiting highrisk areas. (AFDD 3-17)

physical attack

The means to disrupt, damage, or destroy targets through the conversion of stored energy into destructive power. (AFDD 3-13)

physical effect

An effect that physically alters an object or system. (AFDD 2)

policy

Guidance that is directive or instructive, stating what is to be accomplished. It reflects a conscious choice to pursue certain avenues, and not others. Policies may change due to changes in national leadership, political considerations, or for fiscal reasons. At the national level, policy may be expressed in such broad vehicles such as the National Security Strategy. Within military operations, policy may be expressed not only in terms of objectives, but also in rules of engagement (ROE)—what we may or may not strike, or under what circumstances we may strike particular targets. (AFDD 1)

positive control

A method of airspace control that relies on positive identification, tracking, and direction of aircraft within an airspace, conducted with electronic means by an agency having the authority and responsibility therein. (JP 1-02) [Also includes the use of design features, procedures, safety rules, or accident prevention or mitigation measures that reduce the likelihood, severity, or consequence of an accidental or deliberate threat involving a nuclear weapon or nuclear weapon system.] [AFDD 3-52] {Words in brackets apply only to the Air Force and are offered for clarity.}

positive identification

Identification is determined by visual recognition, electronic support systems, non-cooperative target recognition systems, identification friend or foe systems or other physics-based identification techniques. Positive identification does not assume identity solely based on location or adherence to airspace procedures. (AFDD 3-52)

precept

A commandment or direction based on carefully worked out principles and meant as a rule of action or conduct. (AFDD 1)

predictive battlespace awareness

The situational awareness needed to develop patterns of behavior, constraints, and opportunities of geography, topography, culture, environment, and forces that allow us to misdirect, predict, and pre-empt our adversaries. Also called PBA. (AFDD 3-60)

principle

A comprehensive and fundamental law, doctrine, or assumption. (AFDD 1)

procedural identification

Identification is based on adherence to airspace control measures and rules. Identification is assumed to be friendly as long as rules are followed, but identification is assumed hostile if rules are not followed and the suspect vehicle is not otherwise positively identified. (AFDD 3-52)

psychological effect

An effect on the emotions, motives, and reasoning of individuals, groups, organizations, and governments. They are commonly intermediate steps toward behavioral effects. (AFDD 2)

radiological dispersal device

Any device, other than a nuclear explosive device, that disseminates radiation to cause damage or radiation injury. (AFDD 3-40)

reachback

The process of obtaining products, services, and applications or forces, equipment, or materiel from Air Force organizations that are not forward deployed. (AFDD 6-0)

recovery teams

Designated Air Force teams specifically trained to operate independently or in conjunction with rotary wing / fixed wing aircraft, watercraft and overland vehicles. Combat rescue officers (CRO), pararescue specialists and survival, evasion, resistance, escape specialists, provide this capability. Also called RT (AFDD 3-50)

reliability tanker

An air mobility tanker that operates within a given area with no scheduled receiver. It acts as a flying spare should another tanker not be able to pass fuel. Additionally it can be used in emergencies when aircraft that were not programmed to receive fuel require it, i.e. combat disabled aircraft or those in which flight conditions have caused excess fuel burn. (AFDD 3-17)

remediation

Actions taken in response to cleaning up a contaminated site to mitigate effects of environmental contamination on human health and safety, the environment, or the mission. Remediation actions can range from total cleanup, to monitoring of the site, to no action required. These site clean-up activities are performed safely and consistently in accordance with the Air Force Solid and Hazardous Waste Program. (AFDD 4-0)

restricted target list

A list of restricted targets nominated by elements of the joint force and approved by the joint force commander. This list also includes restricted targets directed by higher authorities. Also called RTL. (JP 1-02) [A list of targets that have specific restrictions imposed upon them. Actions that exceed specific restrictions are prohibited until coordinated and approved by the establishing headquarters. Targets are restricted because certain types of actions against them may have negative political, cultural, law of armed conflict or propaganda implications, or may interfere with projected friendly operations. The RTL is nominated by elements of the joint force and approved by the combined force commander. This list also includes restricted targets directed by higher authorities.] [AFDD 3-60] {Words in brackets apply only to the Air Force and are offered for clarity.}

retrograde

> Returning assets—particularly repairable parts—from the area of operations to their source of repair. (AFDD 4-0)

security assistance team

> For purposes of Air Force Foreign Internal Defense doctrine, any team temporarily deployed by the United States Air Force to a recipient country to perform security assistance duties in behalf of the US government. (AFDD 3-22)

security measures

> The means to protect and defend information and information systems. Security measures include operations security and information assurance. (AFDD 3-13)

senior airfield authority

> The senior airfield authority is an individual designated by the joint force commander to be responsible for the control, operation, and maintenance of an airfield to include runways, associated taxiways, parking ramps, land, and facilities whose proximity affect airfield operations. Also called SAA. (JP 3-17, AFDD 6-0)

sequential effects

> Effects that are imposed one after another. Also known as serial effects. (AFDD 2)

sequential operations

> Operations that apply pressure in sequence, imposing one effect after another, usually over a considerable period of time. Also known as serial operations. (AFDD 2)

services

> As related to security assistance, includes any service, test, inspection, repair, training, publication, technical or other assistance, or defense information used for the purpose of furnishing nonmilitary assistance under the Foreign Assistance Act (FAA) of 1961, as amended, or for making military sales under the US Arms Export Control Act of 1976, as amended. (AFDD 3-22)

space assets

> A generic term which may refer to any of the following individually or in combination: space systems, individual parts of a space system, space personnel, or supporting infrastructure. (AFDD 3-14)

space capability

> 1. The ability of a space asset to accomplish a mission. 2. The ability of a terrestrial-based asset to accomplish a mission in space (e.g., a ground-based or airborne laser capable of negating a satellite). See also space; space asset. [JP 1-02] [The ability of a space asset or system to accomplish a mission.] [AFDD 3-14] {Words in brackets apply only to the Air Force and are offered for clarity.}

space control

Combat, combat support, and combat service support operations to ensure freedom of action in space for the United States and its allies and, when directed, deny an adversary freedom of action in space. The space control mission area includes: surveillance of space; protection of US and friendly space systems; prevention of an adversary's ability to use space systems and services for purposes hostile to US national security interests; negation of space systems and services used for purposes hostile to US national security interests; and directly supporting battle management, command, control, communications, and intelligence. (JP 1-02) [Operations to attain and maintain a desired degree of space superiority by allowing friendly forces to exploit space capabilities while denying an adversaries ability to do the same (e.g. protection, prevention and negation). SC is achieved through offensive counterspace and defensive counterspace operations. Note: The Air Force uses counterspace as an equivalent definition of the space control mission.] Also called SC (AFDD 3-14.1) {Words in brackets apply only to the US Air Force and are offered for clarity.}

space coordinating authority

An authority in theater to coordinate joint space operations and integrate space capabilities. SCA can be retained by the JFC but is generally delegated down to the functional component commander with the preponderance of space forces, expertise in space operations, and ability to command and control. (AFDD 3-14)

space force enhancement.

Combat support operations to improve the effectiveness of military forces as well as support other intelligence, civil, and commercial users. The space force enhancement mission area includes: ISR; integrated tactical warning and attack assessment; command, control, and communications; position, velocity, time, and navigation; and environmental monitoring. (JP 1-02) [Space-based capabilities that contribute to maximizing the effectiveness of military air, land, sea and space operations as well as support other intelligence, civil, and commercial users. The SFE mission area includes: ISR; integrated warning and attack assessment; communications; positioning, navigation and timing; blue force tracking; space environment monitoring and weather services.] Also called SFE [AFDD 3-14] {Words in brackets apply only to the US Air Force and are offered for clarity.}

space forces

The space and terrestrial systems, equipment, facilities, organizations, and personnel necessary to access, use and, if directed, control space for national security. (JP 1-02) [Operational military units which consist of some combination of space assets such as space-based and terrestrial equipment, facilities, organizations, and personnel used to exploit space for national security.] [AFDD 3-14] {Words in brackets apply only to the Air Force and are offered for clarity.}

space parity

That condition wherein neither opposing force enjoys an appreciable advantage over the other in controlling the space domain. (AFDD 3-14)

space situation awareness

The requisite current and predictive knowledge of space events, threats, activities, conditions, and space system (space, ground, link) status, capabilities, constraints and employment—current and future, friendly and hostile—to enable commanders, decision makers, planners, and operators to gain and maintain space superiority across the spectrum of conflict. Space situation awareness is the cornerstone of space operations, all-inclusive of space force enhancement, space support, and space control. Also called SSA. (AFDD 3-14)

space superiority

The degree of dominance in space of one force over another that permits the conduct of operations by the former and its related land, sea, air, space, and special operations forces at a given time and place without prohibitive interference by the opposing force. (JP 1-02) [That level of control in the space domain that one force enjoys over another that permits the conduct of operations at a given time and place without prohibitive interference by the opposing force. Space superiority may be localized in time and space, or it may be broad and enduring.] [AFDD 3-14] {Words in brackets apply only to the Air Force and are offered for clarity.}

space support

Combat support operations to deploy and sustain military and intelligence systems in space. The space support mission area includes launching and deploying space vehicles, maintaining and sustaining spacecraft on-orbit, and deorbiting and recovering space vehicles, if required. (JP 1-02) [Those operations conducted with the objective of deploying, sustaining, and augmenting elements or capabilities of military space systems. Space support consists of spacelift, on-orbit support, deorbiting and recovering space vehicles, and reconstitution of space forces.] [AFDD 3-14] {Words in brackets apply only to the Air Force and are offered for clarity.}

space supremacy

That level of control in the space domain that one force enjoys over another that permits the conduct of operations at a given time and place without effective interference by the opposing force. Space supremacy may be localized in time and space, or it may be broad and enduring. (AFDD 3-14)

space system

A system with a major functional component that operates in the space environment or affects a space-based capability. Space systems consist of nodes and links. There are three nodes: space, terrestrial, and airborne. A space system also consists of links: control and mission. (AFDD 3-14)

special operations expeditionary group

An independent group, normally the lowest command echelon of forces reporting directly to a COMAFFOR, JSOTF, JSOACC, or JTF. Also called SOEG. (AFDD

3-05)

special operations expeditionary squadron

The squadron is the basic fighting unit of the US Air Force. Squadrons are configured to deploy in support of crisis action requirements. However, an individual squadron is not designed to conduct independent operations; it requires support from other units to obtain the synergy needed for sustainable, effective operations. As such, an individual squadron or squadron element should not be presented by itself without provision for appropriate support and command elements. If a single operational squadron or squadron element is all that is needed to provide the desired operational effect it should deploy with provision for commensurate support and command and control elements. This squadron is normally subordinate to a special operations expeditionary group or wing. Also called SOES. (AFDD 3-05)

special operations expeditionary wing

Normally composed of a special operations wing or a wing slice. The SOEW is composed of the wing command element and appropriate groups. It is attached to a COMAFFOR, JSOTF, JSOACC, or JTF depending upon size, duration, and nature of the operation. The SOEW may be composed of units from different wings, but where possible, is formed from units of a single wing. Also called SOEW. (AFDD 3-05)

special operations low level

Selected airlift SOLL crews trained to augment core Air Force special operations forces by performing specialized low-level flight. SOLL are limited to a no-to-low threat environment during visual weather conditions. (AFDD 3-05)

specialty training

The total training process (life cycle) used to qualify Airmen in their assigned specialty. (AFI 36-2201 and AFDD 1-1)

spectrum management

Planning, coordinating, and managing joint use of the electromagnetic spectrum through operational, engineering, and administrative procedures, with the objective of enabling electronics systems to perform their functions in the intended environment without causing or suffering unacceptable interference. (AFDD 6-0)

split operations

One type of distributed operations. It describes those distributed operations conducted by a single command and control (C2) entity that is separated between two or more geographic locations. A single commander must have oversight of all aspects of a split C2 operation. (AFDD 6-0)

storage

1. The retention of data in any form, usually for the purpose of orderly retrieval and documentation. 2. A device consisting of electronic, electrostatic, electrical, hardware or other elements into which data may be entered, and from which

data may be obtained as desired. (JP 1-02) [Maintaining information for later retrieval and access by the user. Access to the stored data may be via remote or local means. This access may be by user retrieval or provided automatically by the storage system. Various media exist to store information including magnetic disk, laser optical disk, magnetic tapes, etc.] (AFDD 3-13) {Words in brackets apply only to the Air Force and are offered for clarity.}

strategic assessment

The measurement of effects at the strategic level. Strategic assessment determines whether overall strategy is working and how well the strategic objectives of both sides are being achieved. (AFDD 3-70)

strategic attack

Offensive action that is specifically selected to achieve national or military strategic objectives. These attacks seek to weaken the adversary's ability or will to engage in conflict, and may achieve strategic objectives without necessarily having to achieve operational objectives as a precondition. Also called SA. (AFDD 3-70)

strategic communication

Focused United States Government efforts to understand and engage key audiences to create, strengthen, or preserve conditions favorable for the advancement of United States Government interests, policies, and objectives through the use of coordinated programs, plans, themes, messages, and products synchronized with the actions of all instruments of national power. Also called SC. (JP 5-0) {The planning, execution, and assessment of integrated and coordinated US Government themes and messages that advance US interests and policies through a synchronized interagency effort supported by public diplomacy, public affairs, and military information operations in concert with other political, economic, information and military actions.} [AFDD 3-61] {Italicized definition in brackets applies only to the Air Force and is offered for clarity.}

success indicator

The conditions indicating the progress toward and/or achievement of an objective or end-state condition. Also called SI. (AFDD 3-60)

suppression of adversary counterspace capabilities

Suppression that neutralizes or negates an adversary offensive counterspace system through deception, denial, disruption, degradation, and/or destruction. These operations can target ground, air, missile, or space threats in response to an attack or threat of attack. Also called SACC. (AFDD 3-14.1)

sustainment

The provision of personnel, logistic, and other support required to maintain and prolong operations or combat until successful accomplishment or revision of the mission or of the national objective. (JP 1-02) [The Air Force's ability to maintain operations once forces engage. Sustainment involves the provision of personnel, logistics, and other support required to maintain and prolong operations or combat until successful accomplishment or revision of the mission or of the national objective.] (AFDD 4-0) {Words in brackets apply to the Air Force and are offered for clarity.}

symmetric operations

Operations in which a capability is countered by the same or similar capability. (AFDD 2)

systemic effect

An effect on the entire operation of a system or systems. (AFDD 2)

tactical assessment

The overall determination of the effectiveness of tactical operations. (AFDD 2)

tactical doctrine

Describes the proper employment of specific Air Force capabilities and their inherent assets, individually or in concert with other capabilities and assets, to achieve desired effects and objectives. Tactical doctrine considers particular objectives(e.g. stopping the advance of an enemy armored column) and conditions (threats, weather, terrain, etc.)and describes how Air Force assets are employed to accomplish the tactical objective (B-1s dropping anti-armor cluster munitions, etc.). Tactical doctrine, in the form of techniques and procedures, also gives detailed guidance on how to develop functional capabilities and accomplish combat support tasks (civil engineers repairing facilities, services technicians providing beddown support, etc.). Tactical doctrine is codified as tactics, techniques, and procedures (TTP) in Air Force TTP 3-X series manuals. Because tactical doctrine is closely associated with employment of technology, change may occur more rapidly than to the other levels of doctrine. Also, due to their sensitive nature, some of these documents are classified. (AFDD 1)

tanker airlift control center

The Air Mobility Command direct reporting unit responsible for tasking and controlling operational missions for all activities involving forces supporting US Transportation Command's global air mobility mission. The Tanker Airlift Control Center is comprised of the following functions: current operations, command and control, logistic operations, aerial port operations, aeromedical evacuation, flight planning, diplomatic clearances, and weather. Also called 618 AF/TACC. (AFDD 3-17)

targeteer

Multi-disciplinary specialists highly trained in analyzing targets and developing targeting solutions to support the commander's objectives. (AFDD 3-60)

targeting

The process of selecting and prioritizing targets and matching the appropriate response to them, taking account of operational requirements and capabilities. (JP 1-02). [The part of the tasking process for selecting and prioritizing targets and matching appropriate actions to those targets to create specific desired effects that achieve objectives, taking account of operational requirements and capabilities.] [AFDD 3-60] {Words in brackets apply only to the Air Force and are offered for clarity.}

task force

1. A temporary grouping of units, under one commander, formed for the purpose of carrying out a specific operation or mission. 2. A semi-permanent organization of units, under one commander, formed for the purpose of carrying out a continuing specific task. (AFDD 1)

technical intelligence

Intelligence derived from the collection, processing, analysis, and exploitation of data and information pertaining to foreign equipment and materiel for the purposes of preventing technological surprise, assessing foreign scientific and technical capabilities, and developing countermeasures designed to neutralize an adversary's technological advantages. Also called TECHINT. See also exploitation; intelligence. (JP 1-02) [Intelligence derived from exploitation of foreign material, produced for strategic, operational, and tactical level commanders. Technical intelligence begins when an individual service member finds something new on the battlefield and takes the proper steps to report it. The item is then exploited at succeedingly higher levels until a countermeasure is produced to neutralize the adversary's technological advantage. Also called TECHINT. See also exploitation; intelligence.] (AFDD 2-0) {Words in brackets apply only to the Air Force and are offered for clarity.}

total asset visibility

The capability to provide users with timely and accurate information on the location, movement, status, and identity of units, personnel, equipment, materiel, and supplies. It also includes the capability to act upon that information to improve overall performance of the Department of Defense's logistic practices. Also called TAV. (JP 1-02) [An integrated structure using a command and control process to ensure the quantity, condition, and location of critical assets are visible.] [AFDD 4-0] {Words in brackets apply to the Air Force and are offered for clarity.}

Total Force

The US Air Force organizations, units, and individuals that provide the capabilities to support the Department of Defense in implementing the national security strategy. Total Force includes regular Air Force, Air National Guard of the United States, and Air Force Reserve military personnel, US Air Force military retired members, US Air Force civilian personnel (including foreign national direct- and indirect-hire, as well as nonappropriated fund employees), contractor staff, and host-nation support personnel. (AFDD 2)

toxic industrial material

All toxic material manufactured, stored, transported, or used in industrial or commercial processes. It includes toxic industrial chemicals, toxic industrial radiologicals, and toxic industrial biologicals. Toxic industrial materials produce toxic impacts to personnel, materials, and infrastructure. Also called TIM. (AFDD 3-40)

unintended effect

An outcome of an action (whether positive or negative) that is not part of the commander's original intent. (AFDD 2)

US country team

The senior, in-country, US coordinating and supervising body, headed by the chief of the diplomatic mission, usually an ambassador, and composed of the senior member of each represented US department or agency, as desired by the chief of the US diplomatic mission. (AFDD 3-22)

war

Open and often prolonged conflict between nations (or organized groups within nations) to achieve national objectives. (AFDD 1)

weaponeering

The process of determining the quantity of a specific type of lethal or nonlethal weapons required to achieve a specific level of damage to a given target, considering target vulnerability, weapons effect, munitions delivery accuracy, damage criteria, probability of kill, and weapon reliability. (JP 1-02) [Weaponeering is the part of the tasking process for estimating the quantity and types of lethal and non-lethal weapons needed to achieve desired effects against specific targets.] (AFDD 3-60) {Words in brackets apply only to the Air Force and are offered for clarity.}

weapons of mass destruction

Chemical, biological, radiological, or nuclear weapons capable of a high order of destruction or causing mass casualties and exclude the means of transporting or propelling the weapon where such means is a separable and divisible part from the weapon. Also called WMD. (JP 3-40)